A Year of PRESCHOOL CRAFTS with Patterns

BY
SUSAN PATER AND JOYCE CARR,
REBECCA BENNETT,
KATHLEEN GRAHAM,
AND WANDA PELFREY

ILLUSTRATED BY ROMILDA DILLEY

STANDARD
PUBLISHING
Cincinnati, Ohio

Library of Congress Catalog Card Number: 83-051448

ISBN 0-87239-789-0

CONTENTS

HINTS FOR WORKING WITH PRESCHOOLERS

In order for a craft to become a meaningful part of the session's learning activities, it must be made by the child himself. The more he does on the craft the more interest he will have in it when he takes it home. Don't think that a craft should look good to an adult. Rather, think how it appears to the child—his work, a part of him, neat or not, upside down or rightside up, scribble-colored all over, or with just a few crayon marks.

Have a completed craft to show the children. Tell them only one step at a time. Give help where needed, when asked. Encourage and praise the children for their efforts, not necessarily for their results.

Always remember to put the child's name on his craft. If a child cannot print his own name, help him do this by letting him hold the crayon while you guide his hand.

Patterns

Use carbon paper to trace the pattern you need onto heavy cardboard. Cut this out and then use it to draw as many of the object as you need. Use an X-acto knife to make openings for the lines in the patterns. Glue a large envelope to the inside back cover of this book and store the patterns here when you have finished with them. This will save time and work when you repeat the crafts.

Materials

Try not to use staples on preschool children's crafts. Staples can be dangerous to young children.

Pressure-sensitive or self-sticking seals are recommended for use on Styrofoam and other surfaces that ordinary seals will not stick on. These seals come in a variety of subjects. See page 6 for a list.

All construction paper used in these crafts is the regular 9″ by 12″ size, unless otherwise indicated.

Collect old shirts (adult size) to make simple painting smocks. Cut off the sleeves. Let the children wear them backward, clipped closed with a clothespin. Smocks may be laundered, and paint mixtures that include a small amount of detergent will wash out easily.

Recipes

Make your own finger paint and play dough. Here are some recipes:

For finger paint, mix 1 cup of mild powdered detergent with 1/3 cup liquid starch (or 1/4 cup water). Beat with a rotary beater until mixture is like frosting. (Add more liquid or detergent if necessary.) Add a few drops of oil of wintergreen if desired. Add food coloring last.

Finger paint may also be made with wallpaper paste and water. As you stir, add more paste or more water until the desired consistency is obtained. Powdered tempera may be added as paint is placed on paper, or may be mixed into the entire amount of paint.

To make your own play dough, mix 1 cup flour, 1/2 cup salt, and 2 tsp. cream of tartar in a saucepan. (Do not omit the cream of tartar.) Add 1 cup water, 1 tbs. cooking oil, several drops of oil of wintergreen (optional), and food coloring. Cook, stirring, for three minutes or until mixture pulls away from pan. Knead immediately. Store in an airtight container. This recipe makes enough dough for about six children.

To make a satisfactory glue for young children, stir a small amount of flour into white glue to thicken it to a medium consistency. Pour into small paper cups. Use craft sticks to apply the glue. This is a good choice for children who don't like the feel of glue on their hands. Another good choice is a glue stick or a roll-on glue, available in drugstores and stationery stores.

Correlation

These crafts correlate with Standard Publishing's nursery Sunday-school curriculum, *Discovering With Julie and Jeff*. They have been planned to provide a new craft for a Sunday evening or midweek class for young preschoolers. Since these young children learn from and like repetition, teaching the same lesson a second time can be beneficial. Note the lesson titles in the upper lefthand corner at the beginning of each craft. Make sure these match the lesson your children hear on Sunday morning. Then use several of the learning centers, sing the recommended songs and use the suggested prayer and action rhymes. Tell the story in such a way that the children can let you know what they remember from the morning hour. A new craft will make the lesson complete.

If you do not use Standard's Sunday-school curriculum, these crafts can still be used effectively. Choose a craft that will tie into your lesson theme or concept. Use guided conversation to make the craft meaningful to the children. Substitute your memory verse or Bible words for the ones suggested on a craft.

MATERIALS YOU WILL NEED

Materials listed below are needed to complete the crafts in this book. Those in **boldface italics** are available from Standard Publishing or your local Christian bookstore.

Supplies to Have on Hand:
Construction paper, 9" x 12", assorted colors (#6261 — 50 sheets, $1.95)
Typing paper
Cardboard
Poster board
Glue (#6397 — pint, $3.40; #6398 — quart, $4.65)
Tempera paint and brushes
Jumbo crayons (#6196 — 8 colors, $1.69)
Scissors (for teacher)
Paper punch
Felt-tip pens, assorted colors, wide and narrow tips, permanent ink
Tape—cellophane and masking
Cotton balls
Sponges
Disposable pie pans
Yarn—red, white, other colors
Craft sticks (#6388 — 1,000, $3.95)
Paper fasteners (#6298 — 70, $1.50)
Paper plates
X-acto knife
Chenille wire (#6390 — 100, 12", $3.50)
Plasti-Tak (#7100 — $1.75)
Magnetic strips (#2665 — $1.00)
Newspaper
Stapler
Thumbtacks
Aluminum foil
Glitter
Gummed stars (#1870 — 500, $.98)

Household Items You Will Need:
Styrofoam egg cartons—1 per child
Plastic margarine lids—1 per child
Thread spools—3 per child
Flannel, soft cloth, felt
Straw, hay, raffia, or ravelled brown burlap
Shoe box
Styrofoam cups—3 per child
Rubber bands
Toilet paper rolls and paper towel rolls
Old greeting cards

Pringles lids—1 per child
Small safety pins
Small oatmeal or cornmeal boxes—1 per child
Heavy string or macrame cord
Styrofoam meat or vegetable trays—2 per child
Drinking straws—1 per child
Self-stick labels
3" x 5" index cards—3 per child
White envelopes, personal size—2 per child
Waxed milk carton—1
Spring-type clothespins—3 per child
Plastic liter bottles—1 per child
Plastic gallon milk jug—1 per child

Seals ($.98 each):
Musical Notes (#1938)
Child Activity (#1940)
The Christ (#1943)

Redi-Stix Seals ($.98):
Jesus, Our Savior (#1736)
Creation (#1895)
Children in Action (#1898)
Fall (#1900)
Winter (#1901)
Spring (#1902)
Summer (#1903)
Happy Day (#1917)
Jesus Loves Me (#1926)
Jesus and Children (#1925)
Birth of Jesus (#1927)

Stick-N-Sniff Seals ($1.49):
Flavorful Fruits (#1912)
Fragrant Flowers (#1913)

The Christ pocket cards (#542 — $.08 each, $7.50/100)

Pictures Needed:
Snapshot of each child—autumn and spring
Baby snapshot of each child—winter
Classroom snapshot—spring
Magazine pictures—children and adults interacting, children, faces of children, child helping (1), flowers
Pictures of your church building—1 per child, spring
Bible pictures—birth, boyhood, and manhood pictures of Jesus (from old take-home papers, etc.)

AUTUMN

Bulletin Board for Autumn

LOOK WHAT GOD HAS MADE!

Materials:
Background material—light blue
Construction paper—autumn colors
Snapshot of each child
Thumbtacks or staples
Patterns—leaf, squirrel (pages 33 and 34)

Directions:
Ahead of time, ask each parent for a snapshot of his or her child. Or, take pictures in the classroom. Keep an instant camera handy, if possible, to take pictures of newcomers.

Cover the board with light blue paper or cloth. Cut a large tree trunk from brown paper. You will probably need to make this in several sections. Tack or staple this to the board. (Watch for loose staples!)

Cut many leaves from construction paper. Fasten enough of these to the tree so that each child can find a leaf where he can add his picture. Let the children add more leaves to the tree or on the ground.

Make letters to spell out "Look what God has made!" Put these at the top of the board.

Cut a squirrel from gray paper and add details with a black felt-tip pen. Put him in the tree. Make a hole for the squirrel's nest with the black marker. Add construction-paper birds if you want.

Lesson 1: Wonderful Things to See

GOD'S WORLD

Materials:
Construction paper—light blue, light green, yellow, brown or tan, red or pink
Cotton balls
Glue
Scissors
Patterns—tree, flowers, rabbit (pa   34)

Directions:
Before the session, cut sheets of light blue construction paper in half. Have one 9" x 6" piece for each child. Using light green paper, cut a strip of grass for each child, 1" x 9". Have rabbits, trees, and flowers cut from appropriate colors of construction paper.

Help each child glue his strip of grass at the bottom of the blue paper. (Or, if you prefer, draw a line across the bottom, 1-1/2" from edge, and let the children add green crayon for grass.) Show the children where to glue their rabbits, trees, and flowers. Give them cotton balls to glue in the sky for clouds.

Application:
Point to the various objects in the picture as you say, *"Thank You, God, for making such a pretty world for us to enjoy. Thank You for soft bunnies. Thank You for big trees and for pretty flowers to see. Thank You for the white clouds up in the sky."*

Sing "God's World," (page 31), changing the words to fit the pictures you have just made.

Lesson 2: Wonderful Things to Taste

MY SNACK TRAY

Materials:
Styrofoam egg carton (1 per child)
Crayons (or pressure-sensitive seals)
Permanent ink felt-tip pen
Foods to taste—
    fresh fruit cut in bite-size pieces

small crackers (oyster, fish-shaped, etc.)
miniature marshmallows
cheese, cut in small cubes
sunflower seeds

Directions:

Collect one Styrofoam egg carton for each child. Wash cartons thoroughly. Have fruit and cheese cut in small pieces before class. Use separate containers for each selection of food to taste. Have small spoons in containers.

Let the children decorate the tops of their cartons with crayons or pressure-sensitive seals. Before eating, have the children wash their hands. Then allow them to select a little of each food and place this in the egg spaces. These trays will make snacks more fun (mealtimes, too, for finicky eaters). Suggest to Mom at the end of the session that a muffin tin makes a more durable snack "compartment tray" for little ones for long-term use.

Application:

Remind the children that God has given us many different things to taste and eat. *"Thank You, God, for sweet apples. Thank You for crunchy seeds. Thank You, God, for soft marshmallows."* Mention each food you have.

You may prefer to use foods with contrasting flavors—sweet, salty, sour, bitter, etc. Also include some with pungent aromas if you are talking about the sense of smell too. Try to include a food or two that is new to the children. Encourage them to try a small amount of this.

Caution: Peanuts, popcorn, and other items that are hard to chew, can sometimes cause choking. If you use anything like this, watch the children carefully.

Lesson 3: Wonderful Things to Feel

FUZZY SHEEP

Materials:
White poster board (or corrugated cardboard)
Cotton balls
Glue

Black felt-tip pen
Pattern—sheep (page 35)

Directions:

Before the session cut two sheep for each child and two strips of posterboard, 1" x 2". Glue the strips between the two sheep before classtime. Now the sheep will stand up. The children may draw on the sheeps' eyes and glue cotton to the outer sides of the sheep.

Application:

Use this craft for a lesson on David, on the creation of animals, or on the sense of touch. Talk about how David might have shown his love for his sheep by gently petting them on their heads and backs. Then tell the children to pet their sheep and feel their soft "wool." *"Thank You, God, for soft woolly sheep. Thank You for wonderful things to feel."*

Lesson 4: Wonderful Things to Hear

CYMBALS

Materials:
Plastic lids from 8 oz. margarine dishes
Empty thread spools
Glue
Construction paper—any colors
Seals of children (optional)

Directions:

Before the session cut out construction-paper circles to fit the insides of the plastic lids. Prepare two lids, two circles of paper, and have two spools for each child. In the classroom have the children glue the paper circles into the lids, then center the spools and glue onto the covered lids.

You may want to glue the paper circles and spools

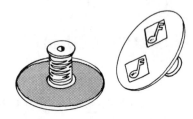

8

onto the lids ahead of time so they will be ready to use at classtime. Let each child decorate his cymbals with seals at craft time, if you so choose.

Application:
Talk about different types of musical instruments. Refer to David's playing the harp. Let the children choose a lively song, and allow them to march and play their cymbals while singing. Say, *"Thank You, God for our voices and musical instruments, like cymbals, that we can praise You with. Thank You for music and other wonderful things to hear."*

Lesson 5: Thanking God for His World

COLORS FROM GOD

Materials:
Tempera paint—red, green, blue, and yellow
Four small sponges
Disposable pie pans
Raw, unpeeled potatoes
White construction paper
Black felt-tip pen
Painting smocks

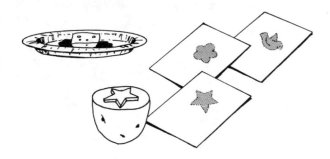

Directions:
Before class prepare paint and store in glass jars to keep fresh until classtime. Pour a small amount of each color of paint in a disposable pie pan. Place a small sponge in each pan of paint. Protect the children's clothing with painting smocks. Give each child a sheet of white construction paper.

Cut potatoes in half and draw the outline of a design on the cut half, if you desire. Cut away the part of the potato around the design. Use a simple pattern such as the flower, star, or bird (page 36). Set the cut part of the potato on the sponge and make a print on paper to show the children how to do this. Have one child at a time make a print in each of the colors. When these are done, hang the papers to dry.

Application:
"Look at the pretty colors you have on your

papers! There's green. God made grass green. Thank You, God, for soft grass to run in. . . . What else did He make green? (Give children time to answer.) Here's blue. Thank You, God, for blue sky to look at. . . . Can you name some other things God made blue? How about red? Yes, red birds and red flowers. . . . Thank You, God, for red birds to see and red flowers to smell. How about a food that is red? Thank You, God, for good red apples to eat." (Continue this way, thinking of things God made in the various colors, and that can be enjoyed by the different senses.)

"Thank You, God, for making colors. And thank You for making such a wonderful world for us to enjoy!"

Lesson 6: God Gives Us Families

FAMILIES HELP ONE ANOTHER

Materials:
Magazine pictures of adults interacting with children
Glue
Black felt-tip pen
Construction paper—1 sheet per child
Pattern—house (page 35)

Directions:
Before the session, cut out pictures that show adults interacting with children. Try to find as much variety as possible—senior citizens with infants, dads with boys or girls, moms with babies, etc. Cut a house shape for each child. During craft time, let each child select two or more pictures and glue them on his paper. Across the top of the paper print "Families Help One Another."

Application:
This craft can be helpful to demonstrate how important our families really are. Make sure you talk about various families—one-parent families, a family that includes a grandparent, an aunt, etc., per-

haps foster parents—whatever is applicable to your children. Say, *"God gives us good mommies and daddies to take care of us, to cook food for us, to wash our clothes, to tuck us in bed at night. He gives us grandpas to play with us and grandmas to read books to us."* Let the children talk about what their families do for them. Then thank God for the various family members—mention them by name if you know them. Sing the "Thank-You Song" and "God Made My Family."

Lesson 7: God Gives Us Friends

OUR BEST FRIEND

Materials:
Red construction paper or felt
White yarn
The Christ pocket cards
Black felt-tip pen
Paper punch
Pattern—heart (page 36)

Directions:
Cut two hearts for each child. Punch 16 holes around the perimeter of the hearts, a little over 1" apart. (Do two hearts together so they will match.)

Cut yarn into 36" lengths, one per child. Dip the ends of the yarn in white glue, twist to a point, and let dry. In half of the hearts cut a 3" slot about 2" from the point of the heart. This will be a pocket when the hearts are sewn together by the children. Purchase *The Christ* pocket cards for each child to slip into his pocket.

At craft time, give each child two hearts (one with the slit), and one piece of yarn. Help the child feed the yarn through the holes to sew the hearts together. When the sewing is completed tie a bow with the leftover yarn. Then let each child slip his picture of Jesus into his pocket.

Application:
Say, *"God has given us lots of friends.* (Let the children name a few.) *But who is our best friend?* . . .

Yes, Jesus is our best friend. Thank You, God, for friends. And, thank You, God, for Your Son Jesus, who is our best friend!"

Lesson 8: God Gives Us Helpers

HELPING PEOPLE

Materials:
Construction paper—a variety of colors
Glue
Craft sticks
Crayons
Patterns—heads and hats (page 37)

Directions:
Cut out two heads for each child, one man and one woman. These need not be in natural colors. Also cut a variety of the hats so the children can choose those they want. In class, give the children their heads and let them pick out the hats they want. Talk about the occupation each hat represents so the children know what they are choosing. Let the children add features with crayons if they want to. Show them how to glue on the hats, then glue craft sticks to the backs of the heads to make stick puppets of them.

Application:
Talk about the job each helper has and how each one helps us. Say, *"Thank You, God, for nurses (or doctors) who help us when we are sick. . . . Thank You for the man who builds our houses and church buildings. . . . Thank You for firemen who put out fires and for policemen who help keep us safe."*

Lesson 9: Thanking God for the People I Know

THANK-YOU TRIANGLE

Materials:
Construction paper
Glue
Felt-tip pen

Adult faces cut from magazines and/or catalogs
Seals—*Child Activity* or *Children in Action,* and *The Christ* or *Jesus, Our Savior*

Directions:

Cut triangles from the construction paper. Make each side 9″ long. Print "Thank You, God," in the center of each one. Have the appropriate seals ready and cut faces of adults from magazines and/or catalogs, at least two per child. If there is a child who lives with grandparents, include older adults in the pictures.

Give each child a triangle and show where to put Jesus' picture first—at the top of the triangle. Then let the children choose the adult faces they wish to include and the seals of children they want. Help them get these in the correct places.

Application:

As the children work, talk to them about the people God has given us—our families, our friends, helpers, and our best friend, Jesus. Lead them in a thank-you prayer for these people.

Lesson 10: God's Care All the Time

CLOCKS

Materials:
Paper plates
Black construction paper
Paper fasteners—1 per child
Black felt-tip pen
Seals of children in action—see page 6
Patterns—clock hands (page 36)

Directions:

Cut clock hands for each child. Mark clock numbers on the paper plates. In class give each child his prepared clock face. Give him several seals that show children doing various things. Help him push a paper fastener through the clock hands and face. Let him spread the fastener apart on the back of the plate.

Application:

Even though the children cannot tell time yet, they are very aware of the purpose and function of clocks. As you assist them in making the clocks, say, *"God gives us daytime and nighttime. And He takes care of us all the time. . . . Thank You, God, for taking care of us during the daytime and at night. Thank You for clocks that remind us of this."*

Lesson 11: God's Care Wherever We Live

GOD CARES FOR SQUIRRELS

Materials:
Construction paper—brown, gray, and black
Empty peanut shells
Glue
Pattern—squirrel (page 33)

Directions:

Cut out a gray squirrel for each child. Also cut a large hole in a sheet of brown paper for each child (see sketch). Hull peanuts so you have two or three half shells for each child.

In class, show the children how to put glue around the perimeter of the brown paper and place it on a sheet of black paper. This will be the squirrel's home in a hollow tree. Let the children glue on the peanut shells for the squirrels' food. They can slip their squirrels in and out of the holes.

Application:

Say to the children, *"God takes care of the little squirrel who lives in a hole in the tree. And He takes care of us—wherever we live—in a little house, a big house, an apartment, in the country, or in the city. Thank You, God, for taking care of us wherever we live."*

Lesson 12: God's Care Wherever We Go

FLYING BIRDS

Materials:
Construction paper—many colors
Yarn
White glue
Paper punch
Branch from a tree (optional)
Patterns—bird and wings (page 38)

Directions:

Before class cut out one bird and one pair of wings per child. Punch a hole near the center of the bird and slits where indicated on pattern. Cut yarn into 15" lengths. Give each child a bird, a pair of wings, and one piece of yarn. Show how to insert the wings in the slits in the body of the bird. Assist the children in securing the yarn in the hole in the birds' bodies. Allow the children to "fly" their birds inside, or, if space is limited, take them outside for a walk.

If you wish, bring in a tree branch and set it upright in a coffee can filled with gravel or dirt. After the children "fly" their birds, let them nest their birds in the tree branch for the rest of the classtime.

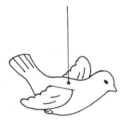

Application:

Sing "God's World." Remind the children, *"God takes care of the birds. When the weather gets cold, some birds fly far away to where it is warm. God helps them know where to go and He takes care of them—wherever they go. . . . He takes care of us, too, wherever we go."*

Let the children tell about trips they have taken and places they have been. Remind them that God took care of them on these trips.

Lesson 13: Thanking God for His Loving Care

"GOD'S CARE" BOOKLET

Materials:
Construction paper
Felt-tip pen
Gummed stars
Seals or pictures of food
Yarn
Paper punch
Pictures of your church building, if possible
Pictures of toys and houses, from magazines
Glue

Directions:

Before class, cut the construction paper in half lengthwise. Lay these two pieces together and fold in half to make a four-page booklet. Punch two holes on the fold and run a length of yarn through and tie in a bow. On the front cover print "God Cares for Us." On the next page print at the bottom, "when we play," then "we eat." On the next two pages print "we sleep," and "at home." On the final two pages print "and away," then "Thank You, God, for Your care."

Provide cutouts of toys for the "play" page, cutouts or seals of food for "eat," gummed stars for "sleep," a cutout of a house for "home," and a picture of your church building for "away." If you prefer, draw a simple outline of a house and church building for the children to scribble-color instead of the cutouts to glue.

Application:

Give the children the cutouts or seals for just one page at a time. Talk about that particular part of God's care, then go on to the next one.

When you have finished, lead the children in "Thank-You Song," page 31, and in the following action rhyme.

GOD IS NEAR

God is near when the sun shines bright,
  (Raise arms above head to form sun.)
God takes care of me all through the night.
  (Rest cheek against hands.)
God is with me when I play,
  (Pretend to push toy truck or dress doll.)
God is with me every day!
  (Clap hands.)

—Mildred Merkel

WINTER

Bulletin Board for Winter

JESUS, GOD'S SON

Materials:
Background material—burlap or paper, perhaps in a dark blue shade
Pictures from the birth, boyhood, and early ministry of Jesus, from teaching pictures or take-home papers (or pictures made from patterns)
Thumbtacks or staples
Construction paper—gold or yellow

Directions:
Cover the board with dark blue burlap or paper. Cut out block letters from yellow or gold paper—"Jesus, God's Son." Place these across the top of the board.

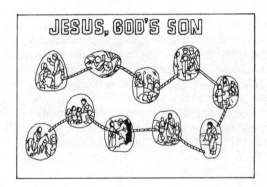

Find pictures that will illustrate each lesson you are studying, from the birth of Jesus, His boyhood, through His early ministry. This will help your children understand the sequence of events in Jesus' life. If you do not have access to pictures, make a simple picture of a person or object that will remind the children of each lesson. For example, an angel for the announcement to Mary, a sheep and/or shepherd for the announcement to the shepherds, a manger and baby for the birth, and so forth. You will find patterns throughout this book to help you with these pictures.

During your lesson time, or perhaps as one of your learning activities, let the children help you put up the picture of the week on the board. As you add these pictures, help the children follow their sequence. Say, *"Last week's story was about Jesus when He was a baby. Now look, He's growing up. He's a big boy, now."* Or you could put all the pictures on the board at the beginning of the quarter and add a piece of yarn each week to connect the new lesson with the one that came before it. Again, emphasize the sequence of events. Small children have great difficulty understanding that the baby Jesus grew up to be the man Jesus. This bulletin board will make a great tool for reviewing the quarter's lessons.

Lesson 1: Happy News From God

GOOD-NEWS LETTERS

Materials:
Construction paper—various colors
Seals—birth of Jesus (see page 6 for list)
Jumbo crayons
Glue
Felt-tip pen

Directions:
Before class, write the following message on sheets of construction paper, one for each child:

"Dear _____:
I learned some very good news today. Jesus was born! I would like you to come to Sunday school with me so you can learn good news about Jesus too!
Love, _____"

In class, make envelopes by folding sheets of construction paper crosswise, leaving 1-1/2" at the tops to make flaps. Help the children glue the sides of the envelopes. Set aside to dry.

Give a letter to each child and let him decorate it with jumbo crayons and/or seals. Fill in the names.

Fold the letters in quarters and insert in the envelopes. Use seals to hold the envelopes shut. Encourage the parents to help their children deliver their letters to friends who do not attend Sunday school.

Application:

Read the letter to the children and tell them, *"You can share happy news with your friends by inviting them to Sunday school to learn about Jesus."*

This "Good News" letter can be used, with a few changes, with any parts of the story of the birth of Jesus—the angel's announcement to Mary, the announcement to the shepherds, or the message in the star for the Wise-men. Or use the idea with other stories about Jesus by changing the message slightly.

Lesson 2: Born in a Stable

BABY JESUS PICTURE

Materials:
Construction paper—brown, white, and blue
Glue
Flannel or other soft cloth
Jumbo crayons
Straw, hay, raffia, or ravelled burlap, optional
Patterns—manger and baby (page 39)

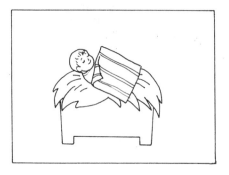

Directions:

Cut a manger-bed and a baby Jesus for each child. Use brown paper for manger and white for baby Jesus. Give each child a piece of blue construction paper. After the children have glued the manger-bed and the baby Jesus to the paper, let them scribble-color the pictures. Have pieces of flannel or other soft cloth, 2" x 3", to use for a blanket for baby Jesus. Glue the bottom end of the blanket to manger-bed so that the cover can be put on and off the baby.

Application:

Use the craft to review the Bible story. Ask simple questions such as, *"Who was Jesus' mommy? . . . Why did Mary and Joseph stay in a stable? . . . Where did Mary put baby Jesus when He was born?"* Sing "Smile, Mary, Smile," and "Jesus Was Born" (see page 31).

Lesson 3: The Shepherds See Jesus

TRUMPETS

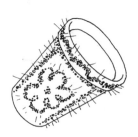

Materials:
Styrofoam cups
X-acto knife (for teacher)
Glitter
Glue
Newspaper
Cardboard boxes (shoe boxes)
Crayons (optional)
Gummed stars (optional)

Directions:

Provide a Styrofoam cup for each child. Before the session cut the bottoms out of the cups with an X-acto knife or other sharp instrument. Give a "trumpet" to each child. Show the children how to spread glue over the outside of the cup, then sprinkle with glitter. (Be sure to put newspaper on the tables for easy cleanup.) Shake off the excess glitter into a cardboard box for reuse. (Optional: Instead of glitter, have the children decorate their cups with crayons and gummed stars.)

Application:

Tell the children, *"We can shout good news through our trumpets, like the angels told good news to the shepherds. Jesus is born!!!"*

Besides using this craft with the story of the angels and the shepherds, it could also be used with such themes as "Jesus Makes Me Happy," or "God Made Me" (or my mouth).

Lesson 4: Gifts for Baby Jesus

STAR VIEWERS

Materials:
Construction paper—various colors
Cardboard tissue rolls—1 per child
Cellophane paper—blue
Gummed stars

Rubber bands
Cellophane tape

Directions:

Give each child a cardboard tissue roll and help him cover it with construction paper. Fasten with cellophane tape. Then give each child several gummed stars and a 4″ square piece of blue cellophane paper. Have the children put the stars on the cellophane paper, then put this over one end of the cardboard tissue roll and hold in place with a rubber band. Show the children how to hold the star viewer up to the light to make the stars "shine."

Application:

Use the star viewer with the story of the Wise-men. Talk about how excited they would have been to see the new star and how long they traveled to find little Jesus. Let the children tell you what they brought Jesus (gifts or presents).

Also use the viewer for a lesson on creation or "God Made My Eyes."

Lesson 5: Thank You, God, for Jesus

TOUCH 'N' FEEL PICTURE

Materials:
Construction paper—brown, dark blue, and white
Craft sticks—4 per child
Chenille wires—1 per child
Straw, raffia, or ravelled burlap
Cotton balls
Glue
Crayons
Patterns—shepherd, sheep, manger, baby (pages 40 and 41)

Directions:

Cut out one shepherd, one sheep, one manger, and one baby Jesus for each child. Give each child a piece of dark blue paper for background, and show where each figure goes. The children may need help, but let them do as much for themselves as possible. Provide crayons for the children to

scribble-color their pictures before adding the touch 'n' feel effects.

Show the children where to glue the craft sticks to make the stable, and how to bend the chenille wire to make a shepherd's crook. Glue this next to the shepherd. Add straw, raffia, or ravelled burlap to the manger, and cotton to the sheep.

Application:

Use the picture to review the story of Jesus' birth. Tell the children, *"The shepherds were happy when the angels told them about Jesus. What did they do? Yes, they went to see the baby Jesus. . . . Jesus' first bed was a manger-bed just like this one. It was in a stable where the animals stayed."* Even though the star and Wise-men did not appear at the manger, you can ask the children a question or two about them for review purposes.

Lesson 6: Jesus Grows Up

GROWING UP

Materials:
Construction paper—several colors
Felt-tip pen
Crayons
Baby picture of each child
Baby pictures from catalogs
Cellophane tape

We grow up...
     just like Jesus did.

Directions:

Several weeks before using this craft, send a note home to the parents requesting that their child bring a baby picture of himself to class. Note: Make sure you have some baby pictures cut from catalogs for visitors or children who forget their pictures.

Give each child a piece of paper and help him trace around his hand on the right side of the paper. Allow children to scribble-color their pictures before you tape the baby photos to the left side. Do not put tape on the fronts of the pictures. Print the words, "We grow up . . . just like Jesus did" on each paper.

Application:

It is difficult for young children to understand that baby Jesus and Jesus the man were the same person. Use this craft to help them understand that baby Jesus grew up the same way they are growing up. This craft could also be used with a lesson on "God Made Me," by changing the caption.

Say to the children, *"Look at your picture as a baby. See how small you were? You couldn't do anything for yourself. Someone else had to take care of you. Now look at how big you are* (point to handprint). *You can take care of yourself. . . . Jesus grew up just like you are growing up."*

Lesson 7: Jesus Heals a Sick Woman

GET-WELL CARD

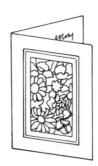

Materials:
Construction paper—various colors
Old greeting cards
Glue
Felt-tip pen
Crayons

Directions:

Collect old greeting cards with flowers or other appropriate pictures for this craft. If you cannot obtain enough greeting cards, use pictures of flowers from seed catalogs or seals with flowers (see page 6 for list).

Fold sheets of construction paper in half and print the following words inside:

"Dear _____,
I hope that you get well soon. I will pray for you.
                           Love, _____"

Give a card to each child and let him choose the picture or seals he wants to use to decorate his card. The children may require help in gluing the pictures. Provide crayons for the children to scribble-color their get-well cards.

If there is someone in the congregation the children know who is sick, such as a child or a teacher, the cards could be collected and given to him. If not, send the card home with the child along with instructions to the parents to help him send the card to a sick friend.

Application:

Read the words inside the card. Tell the children, *"We want to give our cards to someone who is sick. The cards will make him or her feel better."*

Use this get-well card with lessons on loving and caring for one another, prayer, as well as a Bible story about Jesus' healing the sick.

Lesson 8: Five Loaves and Two Fish

FOOD BASKETS

Materials:
Construction paper—various colors
Glue
Crayons
Patterns—basket, loaf, fish (pages 40 and 42)

Directions:

Each child will need a sheet of construction paper, a basket, two fish, and five loaves. Show the children how to put glue on just the outside edges—sides and bottom—of the basket. Make sure the top is open so the loaves and fish can be put inside. Let the children scribble-color their baskets and the loaves and fish.

Application:

Let the children pretend to be Jesus' helpers by passing out the loaves and fish (to dolls, or to each other, or just to imaginary people). Then have them collect the leftovers and place them in baskets. Remind the children that only Jesus could do this because He is the Son of God.

To use this with another lesson, use fruit in place of the loaves and fish for a lesson on "God Gives Food," "Thank You, God, for Food," or "Sharing With Others."

Lesson 9: Jesus Does Wonderful Things

DOORKNOB HANGER

Materials:
Paper plates—dinner size
Felt-tip pen
Seals—*The Christ,* flowers
Crayons

Directions:

Before the session cut holes in the plates, about 2-1/2" in diameter, as shown in the sketch. Print the words "Jesus is . . . the Son of God" on the outside edge of each plate. Give each child a plate and let him scribble-color his doorknob hanger. Provide seals of flowers and *The Christ* for the children to add.

Application:

Talk about the special things Jesus could do because He is the Son of God. *"Jesus fed lots of people with just a little bit of bread and some small fish. . . . He could do that because He is God's Son. . . . Jesus could make sick people well again because He is God's Son. . . . Jesus could do lots of special things because He is God's Son."*

Adapt this craft to other themes by using other Bible words and appropriate seals. Remind the children to hang their pictures on their bedroom doors to help them remember God's Son, Jesus, and the wonderful things He could do.

Lesson 10: A Friend for Zaccheus

ZACCHEUS

Materials:
Construction paper—blue, brown, and white
Tempera paint—green, yellow, and orange
Small pie pans
Spring-type clothespins
Newspapers
Painting smocks
Felt-tip pens
Sponges
Crayons
Patterns—tree trunk, man (pages 38 and 41)

Directions:

Cover tables with newspaper. Provide painting smocks for the children. Before class, cut one Zaccheus figure and one tree trunk for each child. Make a small slit, large enough for the Zaccheus figure, where the leaf area of the tree will be (see sketch). Put paint in small pie pans. Use small pieces of sponge in the spring-type clothespins in place of brushes. Put several of these in each pan of paint.

Before the children paint, help them glue the tree trunks on their papers. They may need some assistance as they begin to dip their sponges into the paint and make "leaves" on their trees. Encourage them to take turns using the different colors of paint.

Pass out the Zaccheus figures and let the children scribble-color them. When the paint has dried on their trees, show the children how to take Zaccheus in and out of the tree.

Application:

The children will enjoy retelling the story of Zaccheus with their pictures. If you omit the Zaccheus figure, the tree can be used with a creation story or a lesson on sharing (emphasize taking turns with the sponges and sharing colors).

Lesson 11: Jesus Loves the Children

"JESUS LOVES THE CHILDREN" MONTAGE

Materials:
Construction paper—various colors
Felt-tip pen
Glue
Catalog or magazine pictures of children
Pocket card, *The Christ*

Directions:
Have enough pictures of children cut from catalogs or magazines so that each child may have several. Give each child a piece of construction paper and a pocket card, *The Christ,* to glue in the middle. Allow the children to choose the pictures they want to put on their montage. As the children choose and glue on their pictures (2's and 3's can use a glue stick without the mess of regular glue), talk about the differences in each child's picture and the fact that Jesus loves every child. Print "Jesus Loves the Children" on each child's montage.

Application:
"Kate has a picture of a little girl with red hair. Jesus loves that little girl. He loves Kate too.... Look at this little boy with brown skin. Jesus loves this little boy too, doesn't He. Yes, and He loves Jeffrey too."

With slight alterations this craft can have many applications. Use with such themes as "God Gives Us Families," (friends, helpers, etc.)—with appropriate pictures.

Lesson 12: Jesus Hears the Children's Song

SONGBOOK

Materials:
Construction paper—various colors

Glue
Music or words to appropriate songs
Felt-tip pen
Seals—*The Christ* or *Musical Note* (optional)
Crayons

Directions:
Fold sheets of construction paper in half to form booklets. Make one for each child. Print on the front, "My Jesus Songbook." If you have copies of old take-home papers that contain music, cut out the music. If you do not have these, print the words to "Jesus Loves Me" and "Praise Him, Praise Him!" (both in public domain) on white paper for each child.

The children may decorate the covers of their songbooks with crayons and/or seals. They may need help gluing the songs inside their books.

Application:
Take some time to sing each song in the booklets. Tell the children, *"Children in the Bible liked to sing songs to Jesus. We like to sing songs for Jesus too. We know He hears us."*

Use this craft with lessons about worship, the senses (hearing), or "Jesus Makes Me Happy." Children can learn that singing is a special way to tell Jesus we love Him.

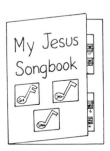

Lesson 13: Jesus Loves Me

"JESUS LOVES ME" MIRROR

Materials:
Paper plates—dinner size
Aluminum foil
Paper punch
Yarn
Felt-tip pen
Glue

Directions:
Before the session, print the words "Who does Jesus love?" on the outside edge of each paper plate. Cut 5" circles of foil for "mirrors" and 10" pieces of yarn for each child.

As you hand out the paper plates, say, *"We're going to make a mirror to see someone Jesus loves."* Help the children glue the foil mirrors to the centers of the plates. Punch a hole in the top of each plate and help each child put his yarn through the hole. Tie the yarn in a bow so the mirror can be hung on a bedpost, a doorknob, or dresser drawer knob.

Application:

Have the children take turns holding up their mirrors as you ask, *"Who does Jesus love? Look in your mirror and you can see."* Continue until each child has had a turn.

This craft can be used to reinforce lessons about Jesus' love—Jesus loves the children, the prodigal son, the lost sheep. Help each child feel special because Jesus loves him. Encourage the parents to use the mirrors with their children at home.

SPRING

Bulletin Board for Spring

WHAT GOD WANTS US TO BE

Materials:

Construction paper—light blue, green, and several pastel shades
Pictures listed below
Staples, thumbtacks, or tape
Felt and cotton, optional
Patterns—sun, bird, cloud, flower (pages 34, 36, and 43)

Directions:

To prepare for this spring bulletin board, take pictures of class members engaged in the following activities:

1. Inviting a friend to Sunday school (talking on a toy phone)
2. Telling a friend, "Jesus loves you" (whispering in a friend's ear or showing him a picture of Jesus)
3. Being thankful for food (praying or eating)
4. Looking at a picture of Jesus
5. Being loved (teacher hugging a child or two children hugging each other)
6. Using one of the senses (smelling a flower, doing an action rhyme, listening to a record)
7. Using hands (playing with play dough or working a puzzle)

Using actual pictures of your class is a good way to tell parents and friends what the children are doing in class. If having real pictures is impossible, however, cut pictures from leftover take-home papers or magazines.

From construction paper, cut seven large flowers (pattern on page 43), in various pastel shades, and enough stems and leaves for the flowers. Print on the petals the following words: Helpers (2 flowers), Thankful (3 flowers), and Learning About Me (2 flowers). Cut a long strip of grass the length of your board and about 4" high. Fringe this. Cut a sun, a bird, and a cloud (patterns on pages 34 and 36). Add cotton to the cloud and make the sun of yellow felt, if you wish. At the top of the board add the words, "What God wants us to be . . ." cut from construction paper or printed on strips of the paper.

Place the first two pictures mentioned above on the "helpers" flowers, the next three pictures on the "thankful" flowers, and the last two on the "learning about me" flowers. Do this at the beginning of the quarter, or add only those that pertain to the lessons from that unit. When the quarter is over, give the pictures to the parents of the children in the pictures.

Lesson 1: Peter Meets Jesus

STICK PUPPETS

Materials:
Construction paper—various colors
Craft sticks
Faces of children cut from catalogs or magazines
Glue
Felt-tip pen
Pattern—puppet (page 42)

Directions:
Before the session, from magazines or catalogs cut out faces of children that will fit on the puppets. Trace and cut out the puppet bodies. Print on the craft sticks, "Come to church."

Help each child glue a face on his puppet, then glue the body to a craft stick, leaving a few inches at the bottom for a handle. Let each child make two puppets.

Application:
When the puppets are completed, encourage the children to play with their puppets. Engage them in dialog by inviting a puppet to come to Sunday school. Remind the children that they are being Jesus' helpers when they invite their friends to come to Sunday school.

The puppets can be used with any Bible story in which there is dialog and/or interaction between two people. Instead of the words suggested above, print the Bible persons' names on the craft sticks.

Lesson 2: Paul and Timothy Are Helpers

"JESUS LOVES YOU" PICTURE

Materials:
Lightweight cardboard
Yarn
Glue
The Christ pocket cards
Felt-tip pen
Paper punch

Directions:
Before the session, cut 6-1/2" squares from the cardboard. Punch holes around the edges, not more than four or five to a side. Cut yarn in 36" lengths. For easy "sewing" wrap tape around one end of a piece of yarn, or dip the end in white glue, twist to a point, and allow to dry. Print on the squares, "Jesus loves you."

Let the children scribble-color their squares if time allows. Help them glue on their pictures of Jesus. Have one end of the yarn taped to the back of each card ahead of time. Help the children "sew" around the edges of their cards. This will take some time for them to do this well. Tape the yarn that is left to the back of the card to make a hanger.

Application:
Talk about how Jesus loves each child, and how each child can tell a friend "Jesus loves you." This picture can be given to an older friend to hang on the wall or to a child to play with.

Lesson 3: Lydia Learns About Jesus

"JESUS' HELPER" NECKLACE

Materials:
Pringles lids—1 per child
Construction paper—various colors
Yarn
Cheerios cereal
Seals—*Child Activity* or *The Christ*
Paper punch
Glue
Small safety pins

Directions:
Cut circles of construction paper 2" in diameter. On each circle print "Jesus' Helper." Cut yarn into 24" lengths. Either tape ends or dip them in glue, twist, and let dry.

Give each child a plastic lid, a circle of construction paper, a length of yarn, and a seal (either from *Child Activity,* or *The Christ*).

Show the children how to glue their circles of paper inside the plastic lids, then add their seals.

Now punch holes at the tops of the lids. Let the children string from 10 to 12 Cheerios on their yarn, add the lid with a safety pin so it will hang straight, then string on 10 or 12 more Cheerios. Help each child tie his yarn in a knot so he can wear his necklace.

Application:
As the children work, talk about being helpers for Jesus. Stress the importance of telling our friends about Jesus and inviting friends to come to Sunday school. Also let the children suggest other ways they can be helpers for Jesus. Use the Bible words, "We . . . are helpers" (taken from 2 Corinthians 1:24), in your conversation with the children.

Lesson 4: I Can Help

CHURCH BUILDING PUZZLE

Materials:
Paper plates—dinner size
Pictures of your church building
Glue
Felt-tip pen
Crayons
Scissors (for teacher)

Directions:
Before the session, print on the outer edges of the plates, "Come to church" (or to Sunday school).

Let the children color their plates, then help them glue on the pictures of your church building. If you do not have pictures, use the pattern of a church

building on page 43. Now cut the paper plates into two, three, or four pieces, depending upon the age and dexterity of the children. Allow time for the children to play with their puzzles. (Mark each piece of a child's puzzle so there will be no mix-up.)

Application:
Talk about why we come to church or to Sunday school and what we do there. Remind the children they are helpers for Jesus when they invite a friend to come to church. Encourage them to share this puzzle "invitation" with a friend.

Lesson 5: Thank You, God, for Jesus

RHYTHM INSTRUMENT

Materials:
Small oatmeal or cornmeal boxes
Heavy string or macrame cord
Spring-type clothespins (optional)
Seals
Tempera paint and wide brushes
Painting smocks

Directions:
Before the session, punch holes, about the size of a pencil, about 1" down from the top on opposite sides of each box. Cut string in 30" lengths. String a piece of cord through both holes and tie the ends together inside the box. Tape or glue on the lid.

Let the children paint their boxes. Allow time to dry. Seals may be added when paint is dry. The clothespins can be used for drumsticks. Fasten them to the cord for easy storage.

Application:
Use this craft for lessons about singing to Jesus or on being happy that Jesus is our friend, as well as a lesson on the sense of hearing.

As the children work on their drums, remind them that Jesus is our friend and that that happy fact makes us want to sing. Give the children time to play their drums and march as you sing (see songs in back of book).

Lesson 6: Breakfast With Jesus

GOOD-NEWS TELEPHONES

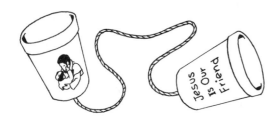

Materials:
Styrofoam cups—2 per child
Yarn
Crayons
Redi-Stix seals—*Jesus, Our Savior, Jesus and Children,* or *Jesus Loves Me*

Directions:
Ahead of time, poke a hole in the bottom of each cup. Cut yarn into 3' lengths. Print on the cups "Jesus is Our Friend."

Let the children decorate their cups with crayons or seals. Make sure that you use pressure-sensitive seals. Ordinary seals will not stay on Styrofoam. Help the children put their yarn through the holes in their cups and knot the ends inside the cups.

Application:
Use this as a craft with lessons about sharing the good news of Jesus with friends. The particular good news in this lesson is that Jesus is alive! Remind the children that children everywhere can be our friends and need to know about Jesus. Let them pretend to call each other and tell the good news—Jesus is alive!

Lesson 7: The Man Who Said Thank-You

DOCTOR EQUIPMENT

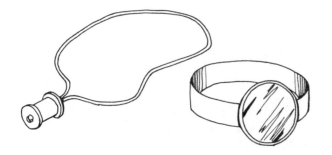

Materials:
Cardboard
White paper
Heavy cord
Empty spools
Foil
Glue
Crayons
Tape

Directions:
Cut cord into 36" lengths. Cut circles of cardboard 3" in diameter. Cut strips of paper 1-1/2" wide and 22" long. Cut foil circles 3" in diameter.

Let the children decorate their spools with crayons. Help them put both ends of the cord through their spools. Tie a large knot in the ends of each piece of cord below the spool.

Help the children put glue on their cardboard circles and attach the foil circles. Then glue these to the paper strips. Fit this to each child's head and fasten with tape. Show the children how to put on their doctor gear and how to use it.

Application:
This would be an effective craft with any of the stories about Jesus' healing the sick or with stories of helpers who take care of us when we are sick. Talk to the children about the fact that doctors help us to stay well and also help us when we are sick. Mention that Mommy and Daddy take care of us, and that Jesus cares for us by giving us good helpers.

Lesson 8: The Lost Sheep

THANKFUL-FOR-CARE BOOKLET

Materials:
Construction paper—various colors
Typing paper
Yarn
Glue
Felt-tip pen
Pictures of people who care for children—parents, grandparents, teachers, policemen, firemen, doctors and nurses, and Jesus
Paper punch

Directions:
Before classtime, cut the construction paper and the typing paper in half. Fold these pieces in half to make a booklet for each child. With a felt-tip pen print "People Who Care for Me" on each booklet. Cut yarn into 18" lengths. Punch two holes in each booklet, on the fold.

In class, let the children select the pictures they want in their booklets. After they have glued the pictures in place, help them put the yarn through the holes in the fold and tie in a bow.

Application:
As the children work, talk about the many ways the different people care for the children. On the last page, print "Thank You, God, for people who care for me."

Lesson 9: Jesus Is Thankful

FOOD TRAY

Materials:
Styrofoam meat or vegetable trays—1 per child
Yarn
Tape
Construction paper—various colors
Glue
Crayons
Patterns—food (page 44)

Directions:
Before the session, print on the tray in crayon, "Thank You, God." Cut yarn in 12" lengths. Cut food from construction paper, using the patterns on page 44. Have one of each for each child. Colors do not have to be natural ones.

Let the children glue the food on their trays. Help them tape pieces of yarn to the backs for hangers.

Application:
Talk to the children about all the good food God gives us. Sing the song "God's World." Sing it several times letting the children sing about a different food each time.

Lesson 10: Arms, Legs, Hands, and Feet

BODY PUZZLE

Materials:
Large paper
Crayons
Scissors
Rubber bands

Directions:
Cut large paper (butcher paper, for instance) in lengths that will be long enough for the children to lie down on them. On each piece print "God made us."

In class, have a child lie down on his piece of paper while you trace around his body with crayon or felt-tip pen. Then let the child color the picture to match his own coloring and clothing. Cut the "body" into pieces so that it becomes a puzzle. Remember to keep this simple. Let the children have time to put their puzzles together several times. Roll up the puzzles and hold together with rubber bands to carry them home.

Application:
As the children work, talk about their hands, their arms, etc., and what they do. Make sure you emphasize that God made those parts. *Thank You, God, for strong legs and arms, hands and feet.*

Lesson 11: My Five Senses

FIVE-SENSES TRAY

Materials:
Styrofoam meat or vegetable trays—1 per child
Tape
Glue
Small bells—1 per child
Chenille wire
Raisins or wrapped candy
Cotton balls
Perfume or lemon juice

Rocks, pinecones, pieces of velvet, sandpaper
Stick-N-Sniff seals—see page 6 for list

Directions:

Ahead of time, print on the trays, "God made our senses." Cut chenille wire in very short pieces. Punch two small holes in each tray, about 3/4" apart. Bend the chenille wire in half and push an end of the wire through the holes in a bell. Now push the ends of the wire through the two holes in a tray and twist the wire securely on the back of the tray. Do all this before class.

Help the children glue or tape on the items mentioned above. Have the raisins wrapped in a small piece of plastic wrap or else use wrapped candy for something to taste. If you use candy, tell the children they can take this home and have a treat at home.

Let the children have time to see, touch, smell, hear, and taste (raisins).

Application:

As the children explore the things on their tray, talk about other things our eyes can see, our noses can smell, etc. Talk about the fact that God made our senses and each one is important. Do the action rhyme below with the children.

My Eyes, My Ears

My eyes, my ears, my nose, my mouth,
My hands and feet so small,
My arms, my legs, my tummy, my head—
I know God made them all!
(Point to each part of the body as you name it.)
—Sylvia Tester

Lesson 12: My Feelings

FEELINGS FRAME

Materials:
Paper plates
Crayons
Paper towel rolls—1/2 per child
Felt-tip pen

Directions:

Before the session, cut 5" circles out of the middle of each plate, and cut a 1" slit at an angle in each paper towel roll. (If you do not have enough paper towel rolls, use toilet paper rolls. Do not cut these in half.) On the plate print, "God made my feelings."

Let the children decorate their plates and rolls with crayons. Help them insert the plates in the slits in the paper towel rolls.

Application:

Talk about feelings that are familiar to the children—hate, anger, happiness, sadness, etc. When their frames are complete, let them take turns looking through the holes and making faces that show certain feelings. Have the other children guess what feelings they are. Let the children know that everyone gets angry, sad, etc., at times because God made us that way. He knows how we feel because He made us. But He does expect us to control our anger, and not feel sad all the time, and so forth. We can talk to God about these feelings and ask Him to help us not feel sad or angry.

Lesson 13: Wonderful Me

"GOD MADE ME" PENNANT

Materials:
Construction paper—various colors
Drinking straws—1 per child
Seals—*Happy Day*
Snapshot of each child
Felt-tip pen
Paper punch
Pattern—pennant (page 44)

Directions:

Several weeks ahead, ask each child's parents for a snapshot of the child to use on this craft. Before the session, cut out the pennants. Punch holes for the straws as shown. On the backs of the pennants print "God made . . ."

Help each child glue on his picture. Print his name next to his picture. Let him add a happy face seal, then put the straw through the holes.

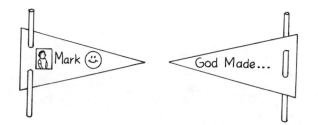

Application:

Talk to the children about the fact that God made them and each one is special. You might want to go around the group naming something special about each child—Mark's nice smile, Kristen's curly hair, David's strong legs, etc. Make sure you mention something positive about each one. Then thank God for each child when you have finished.

SUMMER

Bulletin Board for Summer

WE SHOW OUR LOVE FOR GOD

Materials:
Cloth or crepe paper
Construction paper
Thumbtacks or staples
Felt-tip pen
Picture of a child helping (from magazine)
Patterns—church building, boy, girl, heart, Bible, and praying hands (pages 36, 45—48)

Directions:

Use a bright color of material or crepe paper for the background. Cut flowers for the border. See page 32 for suggestions on how to do this. From construction paper cut a simple church building, a path, and a boy and girl. Use the patterns on pages 45 and 47 for these.

Cut stems and leaves for the large flowers. Use the large heart pattern (page 36) for the flowers.

As you begin a new unit, place a picture on one of the heart-flowers. Start with a Bible (page 46), then the praying hands (page 48), and finally, a picture of a child helping (from a magazine).

Cut the words "We Show Our Love for God" in large black letters (see page 32), or print them on strips of paper.

Lesson 1: Ezra Reads About God

BIBLE WALL HANGING

Materials:
Felt or burlap—any color
Felt—black
Craft sticks—1 per child
Yarn—red and any other color
Permanent-ink felt-tip pen
Glue

Directions:

Before classtime, notch the craft sticks about 3/8" from each end. Cut the felt or burlap into pieces 3" x 6", one for each child. Turn down 1" of the material and glue to make a pocket for the craft sticks.

Cut 1" x 1-1/2" pieces of black felt. Cut 3" pieces of yarn (any color) and 1" pieces of red yarn. For each child, glue one of the pieces of red yarn to the right side of a piece of the black felt, leaving an end of the yarn hanging below the felt. Print the Bible words "Love . . . God" on the large pieces of cloth (see sketch).

During class, allow the children to glue their "Bibles" on the hangings, yarn-side down. Help them slip their craft sticks into the pockets and then tie the yarn hangers on both ends of the sticks, at the notches.

Application:

"God gave us the Bible so we could learn how He wants us to live. The Bible teaches us how to treat our friends, to mind our parents, and to love God.... This wall hanging has the Bible words, 'Love...God' on it. Take it home and hang it up. Ask Mommy or Daddy to help you learn these words."

This wall hanging can be made to fit any theme by changing the words on it.

Lesson 2: Jesus Reads About God

ENVELOPE BIBLE

Materials:
White envelopes—personal size
Labels or paper
Glue
Index cards—3" x 5"
Felt-tip pen

Directions:

Ahead of time, print or type HOLY BIBLE on the labels (or on plain paper). On the index cards print the Bible words for the quarter. Date the cards so parents will know which words are being taught each unit.

Show the children a Bible with HOLY BIBLE printed on the cover. Let them position their labels on the envelopes to make them look like the fronts of Bibles. Give each child the cards with the Bible words printed on them.

Application:

"We cannot learn from the Bible unless we look inside. Mommy, Daddy, or Teacher can open the Bible and read what it says. You need to listen and remember. ... You have put some Bible words in your pretend Bible. Take them home and let Mommy or Daddy help you learn them. Say them often this week."

This can be used with any Bible words. It can also be used with the story of Jesus using the Scriptures to resist temptation.

Lesson 3: Timothy Hears Bible Stories

BIBLE MEGAPHONE

Materials:
Heavy construction paper or lightweight cardboard
Waxed milk carton
Tempera paint
Large bristle brush
Painting smocks
X-acto knife
Patterns—megaphone and BIBLE (page 48)

Directions:

Before class make a stencil using the pattern on page 48. Use a piece of a waxed milk carton for the stencil. Cut it with an X-acto knife. Cut the cardboard megaphones. Draw a straight line on each megaphone and print the words "learns from the" under it (see sketch).

During class print each child's name on the line on his megaphone. Allow the children to use the stencil to print the word *Bible* under your printed words. Work with one or two children at a time. Make sure their clothes are protected by painting smocks. As the paint begins to dry, help the children tape their megaphones into shape.

Application:

"People sometimes use a megaphone to talk through when they want to be heard above a lot of noise. You children listen well, so I don't have to raise my voice or use a megaphone to make you hear what the Bible has to say.... Can you say your Bible words through your megaphones?"

Use this megaphone craft with any Bible story about preaching or talking, such as Peter's preaching on Pentecost (Acts 2) or Elijah on Mt. Carmel (1 Kings 18:20-40).

Lesson 4: Philip's Friend Reads About Jesus

FLANNEL FACE

Materials:
Flannel or felt—2 colors
Envelopes—1 per child

Glue
Yarn—red
Patterns—head and features (page 46)

Julie Beth Learns
from the Bible
to
"Love...God" Mark 12:30

Directions:

Cut heads from flannel or felt, one for each child. Make sure the girls' heads have the longer hair. Cut eyes, nose, and ears from second color of flannel or felt. Print "_____ learns from the Bible to 'Love . . . God' " at one end of the envelope.

During class print each child's name in the blank as you give out the envelopes. Help the children glue the heads on the envelopes. Give out the face parts and let the children arrange them. After they have played with them for a while, show the children how to store the parts in the envelope for later play.

Application:

"We have been talking about learning from the Bible. You learn in many ways. You use your ears to listen (add ears). *You use your eyes to see pictures and other things I show you* (add eyes). *You use your nose to learn smells* (add nose). *You use your mouths to ask questions and to say Bible words* (add mouth). *Even though you are not yet old enough to read the Bible, there are many ways you can learn from it."*

This craft can be adapted to fit a lesson on creation (God made our eyes, etc.), or one on the senses. You could also make the members of a family by enlarging the patterns (or reducing them slightly) to make the various ages of people in the family.

Lesson 5: The Bible Teaches Me

SWITCH-PLATE DEVOTIONAL REMINDER

Materials:
Self-adhesive plastic—2 colors
Permanent-ink felt-tip pen
Patterns—switch plate and flowers (pages 46 and 47)

Directions:

Before class cut the switch-plate covers from one of the shades of self-adhesive plastic. Cut the flowers (three per child) from the second color. Print the words "Read the Bible" on the flowers, one word per flower. Note: If your children are all very young, print the words on the cover after they have attached one or more flowers.

In class give out the flowers in the order in which the words appear. Help the children remove the backing from the flowers and apply them to the switch-plate cover. Tell them to have Mommy or Daddy stick the cover over the switch plate in their rooms. (You may want to send home a note to this effect.)

Application:

"We know we should read the Bible, but sometimes we forget. If you stick this over the switch plate in your room, Mommy or Daddy will remember to read the Bible with you."

This can be used with any appropriate message or memory verse.

Lesson 6: Jesus Talks to God

HANDPRINT PILLOW TOP

Materials:
Plain fabric (cotton or cotton blend)
Tempera paint
Permanent-ink felt-tip pen
Painting smocks
Materials for washing up

Directions:

Before class cut the fabric into 9" squares. Print "can pray" along one side, using the permanent-ink felt-tip pen.

During classtime, allow one child at a time to put on a painting smock, place a hand in the paint, and carefully lay it down (thumb up) on his or her square material. It will speed things up if one teacher prints the child's name and helps with the handprint, and the other teacher helps the child clean the paint from his hand and remove the smock. You may want to send a note home saying that the top can be stitched into a pillow top, though the tempera paint will not be permanent. Parents may prefer to frame this or mount it on poster board. This could be trimmed with a simple braid glued around the edge.

Application:

"Jeffrey, you can talk to God just like Jesus did. Your handprint looks like praying hands. It will remind you to talk to God."

This can be used with any lesson on prayer, such as Hannah's prayer (1 Samuel 1, 2) or Daniel's praying (Daniel 6).

Lesson 7: A King Prays for Help

PRAYER SPINNER

Materials:
Poster board—2 colors
Seals or pictures of things to pray for
Glue
Paper fasteners—1 per child
Pattern—arrow (page 36)

Directions:

In preparation for class, cut out circles of poster board, 8" in diameter. Cut arrows from the second color of board. Put small holes in the center of the circles and in the ends of the arrows. Find pictures of things a person can pray for, or have appropriate seals ready. (For example, *Creation,* or *Summer*.) Separate the pictures into categories.

Show the children your sample prayer spinner. Let them choose pictures of things they would pray for. Help them glue the pictures around the edge of the circle. Give a paper fastener to one child at a time

and help him put it in the hole in the arrow and then into the hole in the circle. Let him spread the ends on the back of the circle.

Application:

"Sometimes when we talk to God we forget what we are going to pray about. Our prayer spinner will help us remember. We can move the arrow to each item."

By changing the pictures slightly, this craft can be used with lessons about things we can be thankful for, and ways the children can help.

Lesson 8: Friends Pray for Peter

PRAYER REMINDER

Materials:
Poster board
Strip magnets
Spring-type clothespins—1 per child
Paper
Pattern—praying hands (page 48)
Glue

Directions:

Ahead of time, trace the praying hands onto poster board, one for each child. Or, if you prefer to make this more personal, cut circles, about 5" in diameter, and trace around the childs' hands in class. Do not cut these out. Print "Pray for" on slips of paper.

Help each child glue his praying hands to a clothespin. Show him how to put the hand face down on the table, apply glue to the top half of a clothespin, then place it on the hand and hold in place for a few minutes. Give each child a piece of strip magnet. Show him how to remove the paper backing from it and press it in place on the clothespin. Demonstrate how the prayer reminder will hold to a metal surface.

Application:

"Maybe Mommy or Daddy needs help remembering who or what to pray for. This prayer reminder will be helpful. It can be put on the refrigerator."

By changing the praying hands to a flower (pattern on page 36), and gluing a child's picture in the center, you can have a recipe holder or message holder for a welcome gift.

Lesson 9: I Talk to God

CARDBOARD TELEPHONE

Materials:
Poster board—5" x 7" for each child
Toilet tissue roll—1 per child
String or cord
Felt-tip pen

Directions:
Before classtime, draw a circle on the cardboard or poster board and print the words "I can talk to God" on it. Punch a hole in the side of the cardboard and one in the end of the tube. Prepare enough for all the children.

In class allow the children to scribble-color the cardboard and tube. Help them attach the string through both holes.

Application:
"Do we need a telephone to talk to God? . . . Of course not. But the telephone will remind us to talk to God every day, at any time of the day. . . . Ask Mommy or Daddy to hang this up where you can play with it. When you do, you will remember that you can talk to God."

Use this craft with any lesson on prayer, as well as with a lesson on telling people about Jesus.

Lesson 10: Jesus Helps a Little Boy

JUMBO GET-WELL CARD

Materials:
Poster board—2 large rectangles
Masking tape
Felt-tip pen
Glue
Magazine pictures of flowers, or seals of flowers

Directions:
Ahead of time, print the words "Get well soon" on the card. Tape the two pieces of poster board together along one of the long edges.

In class, let the children glue flowers (or place seals) on the front of the large card. When they feel they have decorated the front of the card enough, help them print their names on the inside. (Let each child hold the pen and you guide him.)

Note: Make sure the card is delivered right away. Perhaps there is a sick or shut-in person the children know who should be the recipient of the card. It is good to tell the children ahead of time where the card is going.

Application:
"When someone is not feeling well, we cannot make him well the way Jesus did the little boy. We can make the sick person feel happier by sending him a card. _____ is sick at home (or hospital). Do you think this big card will make him feel happier? I think it will."

Lesson 11: A Lady Who Helped

LITER LITTER BOTTLE

Materials:
Liter-size plastic bottles—1 per child
Labels—pressure sensitive ones
Redi-Stix seals—see list on page 6
Yarn

Directions:
Before class cut a hole about 3" or 4" in diameter

29

in the bottle, leaving the neck of the bottle intact. On a plain label print the words "Help keep God's world clean."

In class let the children put the labels and decorative seals on the bottle. Help them put the yarn through the two openings in the bottle and tie. This will provide a handle for the litter bottle.

Application:
"There are many ways we can help others. One way is to keep our part of the world clean for everyone. Take your bottle home and use it to clean up litter around your yard."

Also use this craft with a lesson on ecology or a lesson on creation and our part in taking care of it.

Lesson 12: Church-Friends Send Help

MILK-CARTON WATERING CAN

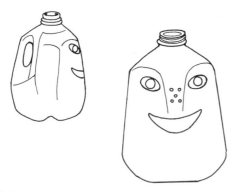

Materials:
Plastic milk carton with handles—1 per child
Ice pick
Colored self-adhesive plastic
Patterns—facial features (page 46)

Directions:
Cut out eyes and smiles from self-adhesive plastic. With an ice pick poke holes in the corner of each plastic jug, opposite the handle.

Show the children how to make a happy face by sticking on the self-adhesive mouth below the holes in the plastic jug and the eyes on either side of the holes.

Application:
"We can help people in ways other than giving money. Do you ever help Mommy water her flowers? This happy-face watering can will help you do this.

Make sure you only water the flowers when Mommy asks you to." (You may want to demonstrate by watering classroom plants.)

Use this also with lessons on creation or lessons on God's care.

Lesson 13: How I Help

"DUSTY" DUSTING MITT

Materials:
Soft, flannel-like cloth
Needle and thread or sewing machine
Felt
Glue
Yarn
Patterns—mitt and features (page 47)

Directions:
Before classtime, from a soft, flannel-like cloth, cut two pieces from the mitt pattern for each child. Cut two eyes and a 2" piece of yarn for the mouth. Place the eyes and mouth in envelopes or sandwich bags. Stitch the mitts together along the curved edges, leaving the straight wrist edge open. If you cannot stitch these, use a white glue around the edges. Give them adequate time to dry.

Let each child glue the eyes and mouth to his dusting mitt.

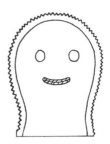

Demonstrate how to dust with the mitt. It will be more successful if the child wears the face side on the back of his hand.

Application:
" 'Dusty' dusting mitt likes to help around the house. Do you think he should have a happy face or a sad face? Ask Mommy if she will help you learn how to dust so you can be a happy helper."

This can be used with any lesson on helping or on the home.

PRESCHOOL SONGS

Smile, Mary, Smile

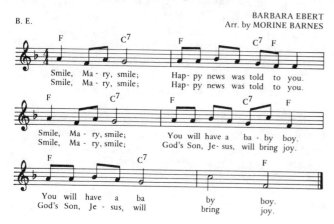

Jesus Was Born

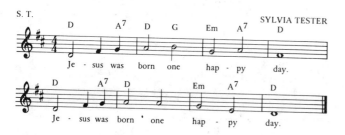

The Shepherds Walked on Tiptoe

Jesus Is God's Son

God Made My Family

Thank-You Song

God's World

We Thank You, Thank You, God

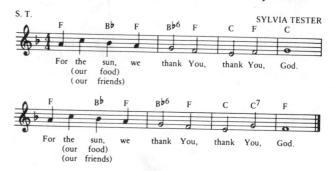

HOW TO CUT LETTERS AND BORDERS

Patterns for Cutting Borders

Decide upon the width you want your border to be. Then cut strips of paper into this width. If pattern needs to be enlarged, do this according to directions on page 33. Fold your strips of paper so that you end up with the right size for the pattern. For example, if you plan to use the tulip design, cut paper 2″ wide and 12″ long. Fold into six equal pieces. Lay pattern so sides touch folds and draw around it. Then cut out, making sure that you do not cut on the folds. Make enough of these to fit around the edge of your bulletin board or whatever you are using.

Patterns for Cutting Letters

The patterns below will guide you as you cut out letters freehand, or you may use them to make cardboard patterns for cutting out letters. (Use lightweight cardboard and a razor blade or X-acto knife.) The size of the paper you use will determine the size of your letter. Large letters are often needed for posters and bulletin boards.

Have or cut all pieces of paper the same size before you begin. Corners may be rounded, if you prefer.

For "F"—cut the lower leg off an "E."

For "G"—add a tip to a "C."

For "Q"—add a slanted tip to bottom corner of an "O."

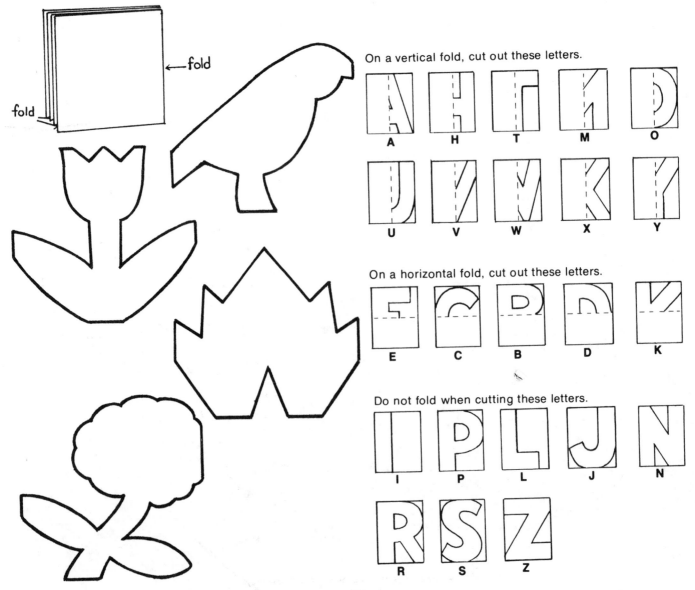

fold

fold

On a vertical fold, cut out these letters.

A H T M O

U V W X Y

On a horizontal fold, cut out these letters.

E C B D K

Do not fold when cutting these letters.

I P L J N

R S Z

How to Enlarge a Pattern

There may be times when you wish to enlarge a pattern. Divide the original pattern into one-inch squares. Divide a larger piece of paper into two-inch, three-inch, or four-inch squares, depending on how much you want to enlarge the pattern. Then copy the original pattern square by square onto the larger sheet.

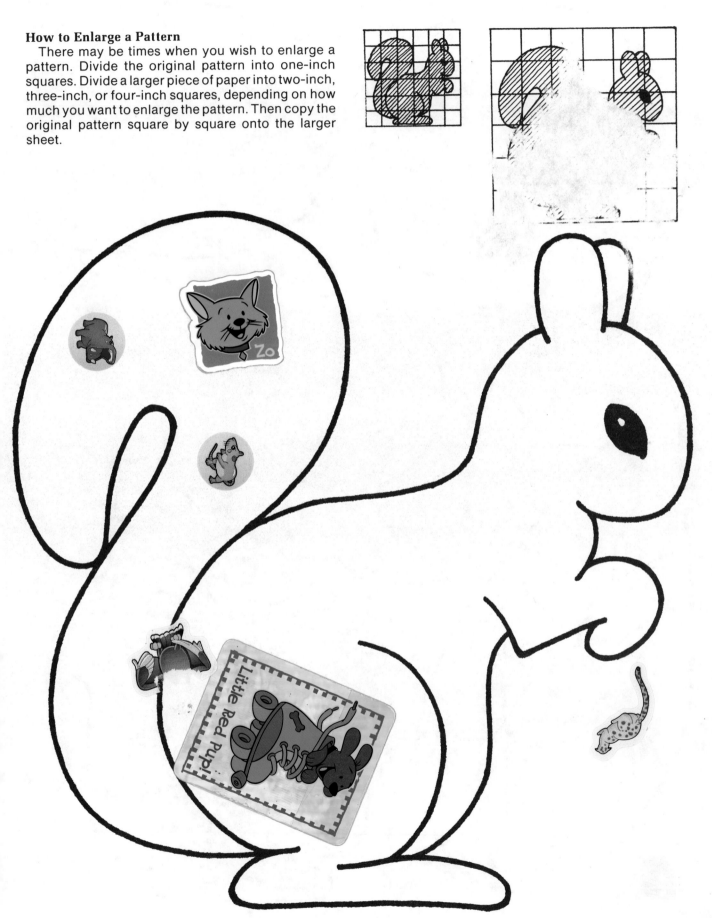

For lesson 1, autumn.

For bulletin board, autumn.

For lesson 6, autumn.

For lesson 3, autumn.

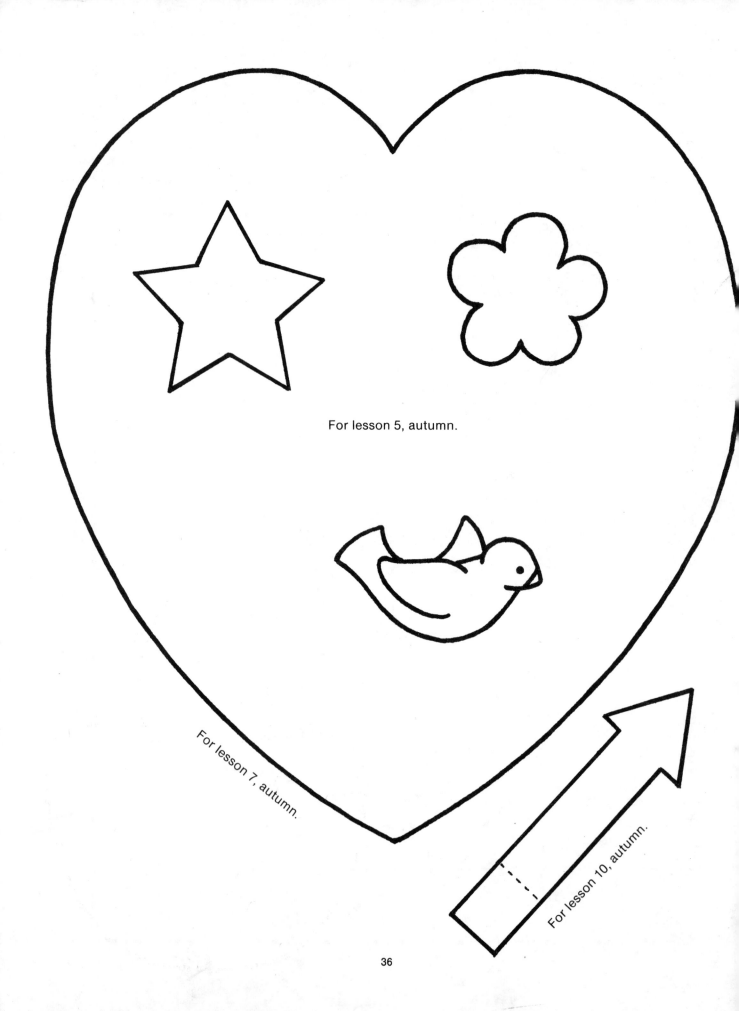

For lesson 5, autumn.

For lesson 7, autumn.

For lesson 10, autumn.

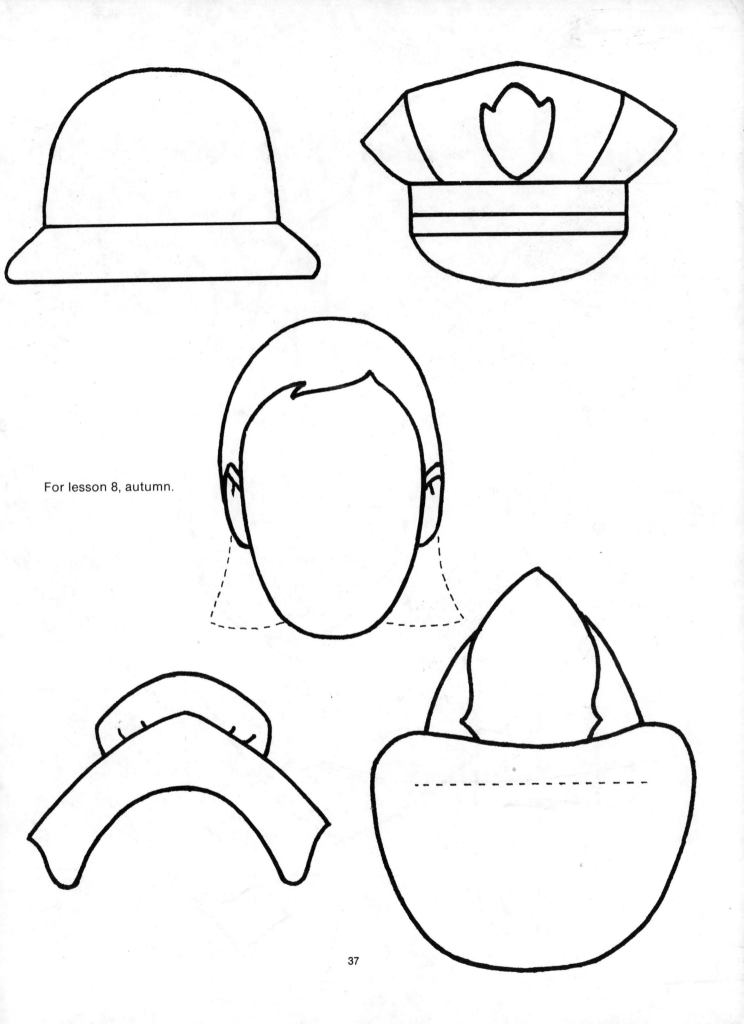

For lesson 8, autumn.

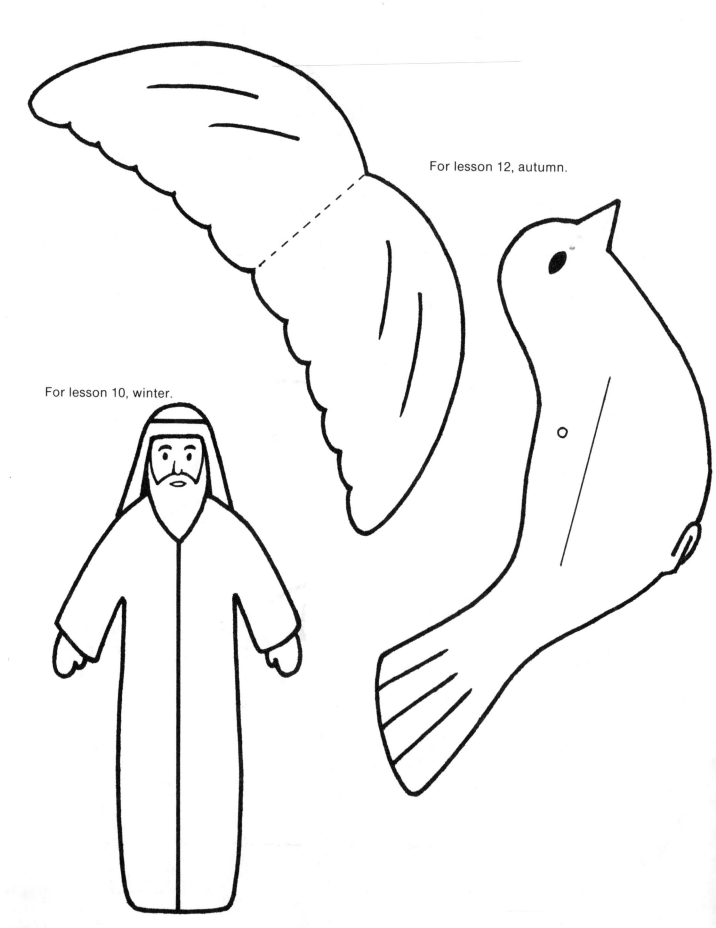

For lesson 12, autumn.

For lesson 10, winter.

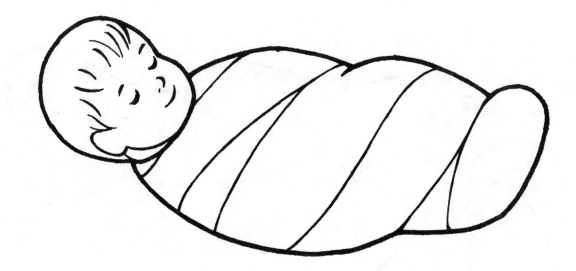

For lesson 2, winter.

For lesson 8, winter.

Place on fold.

For lesson 5, winter.

For lesson 10, winter.

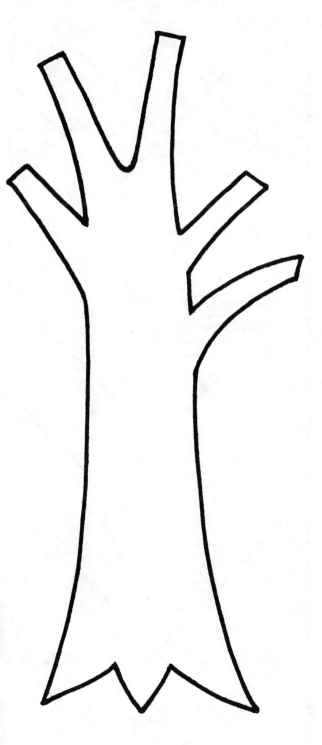

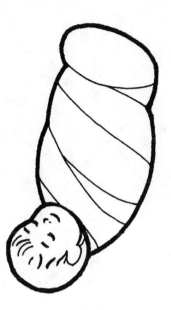

For lesson 5, winter.

For lesson 1, spring.

For lesson 8, winter.

For bulletin board, spring.

For lesson 4, spring.

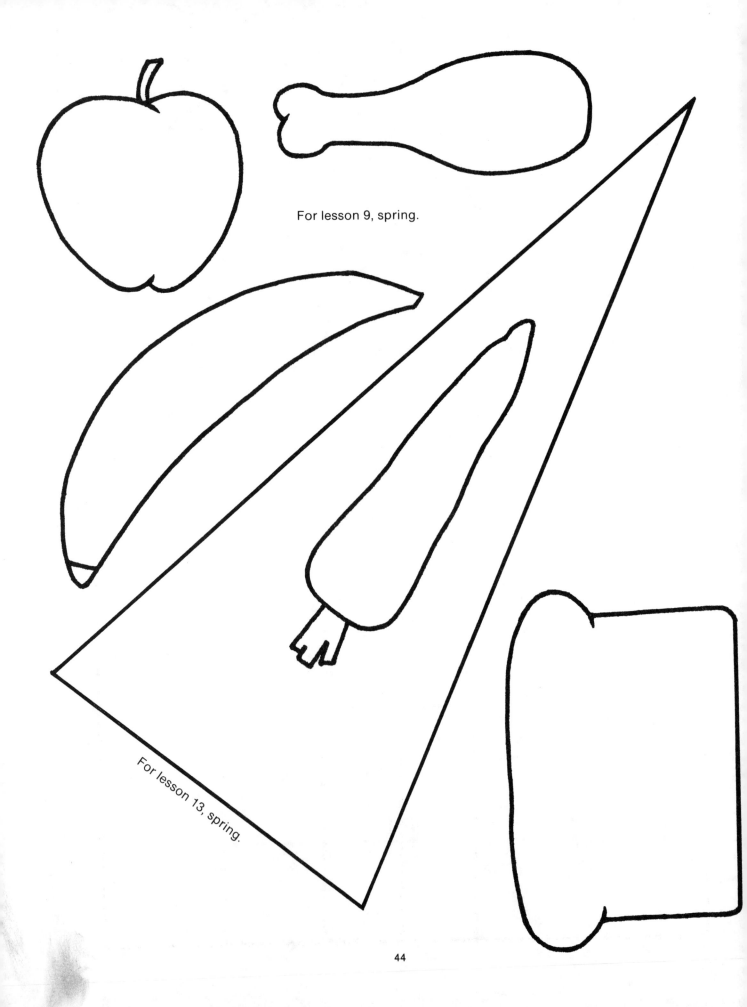

For lesson 9, spring.

For lesson 13, spring.

For bulletin board, summer.

For lesson 12, summer.

Bible

For bulletin board, summer.

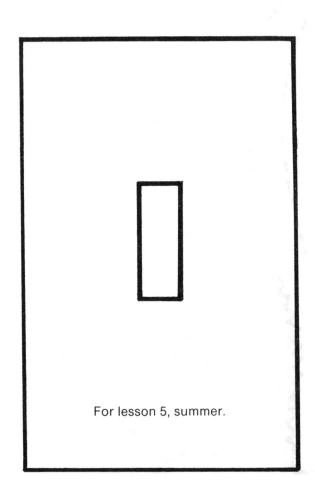

For lesson 5, summer.

For lesson 4, summer.

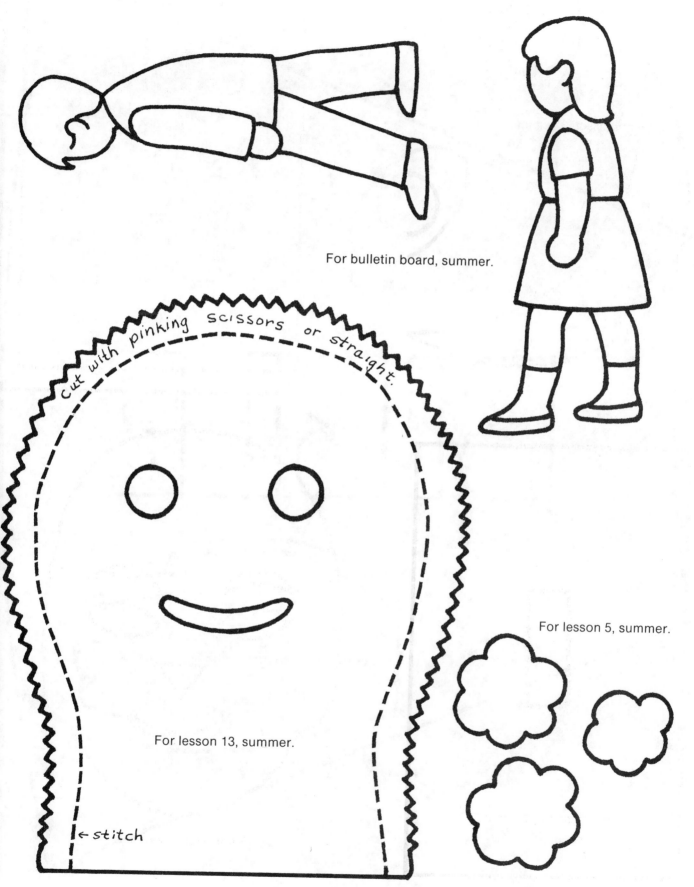

For bulletin board, summer.

Cut with pinking scissors or straight.

For lesson 5, summer.

For lesson 13, summer.

← stitch

For lesson 3, summer.

BIBLE

For lesson 8 and for bulletin board, summer.